Demons and Angels

Coloring Book

Adult Colouring Books

Aryla Publishing 2020

978-1-912675-88-3

www.arylapublishing.com

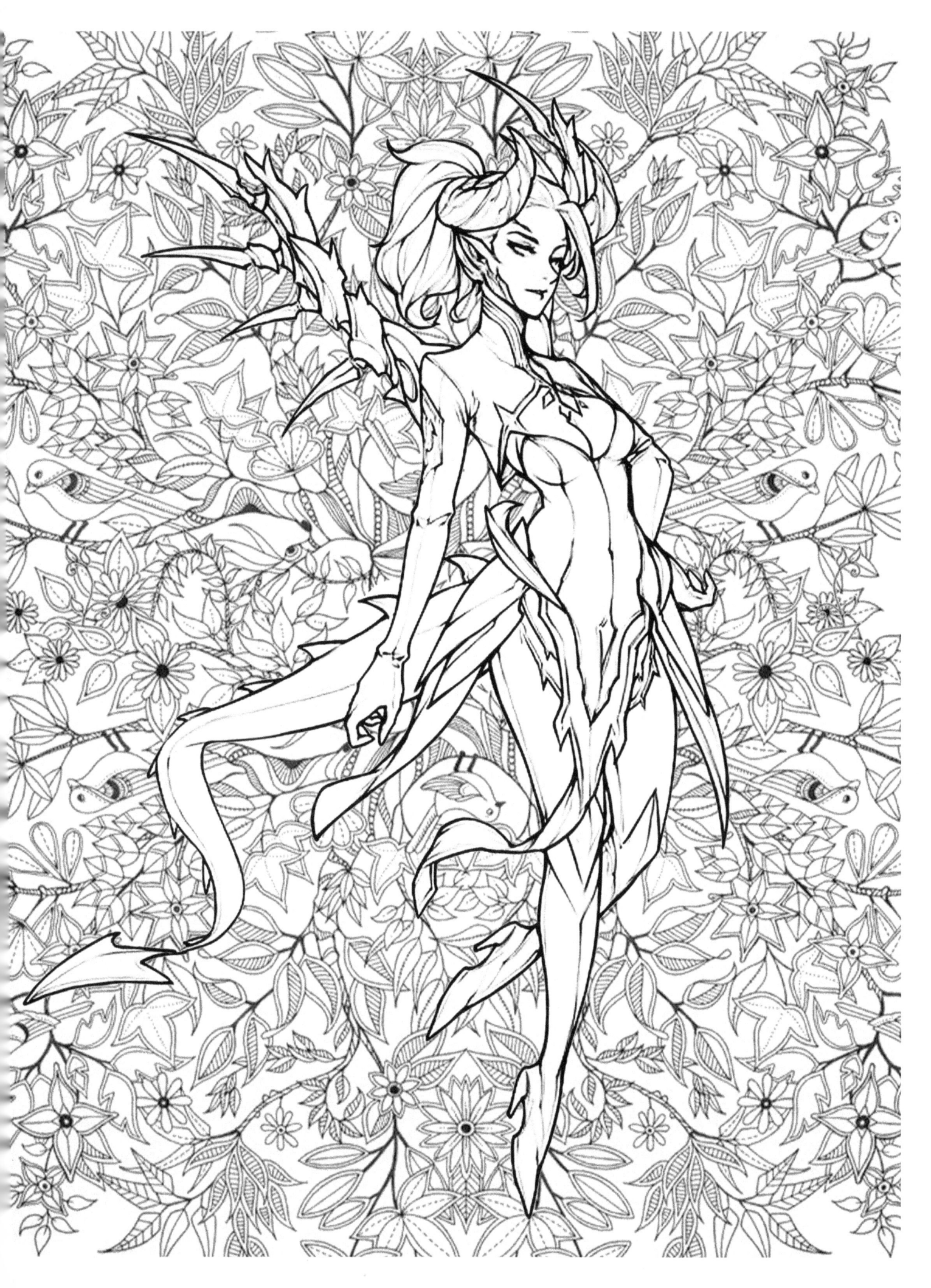

Thank you for purchasing this book.

If you would like to know more about Aryla Publishing Books please visit:-

www.ArylaPublishing.com

Or follow us on
Facebook
Twitter
Instagram
for *free promotions*

@arylapublishing

We would love to know what you think of this book so please leave us a review.

Have a wonderful day ☺

Other Coloring Books from Aryla Publishing

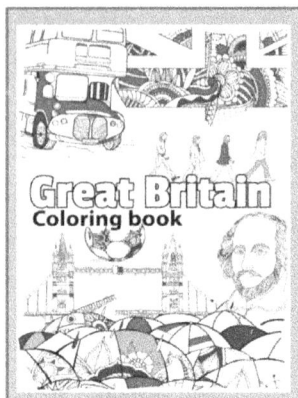

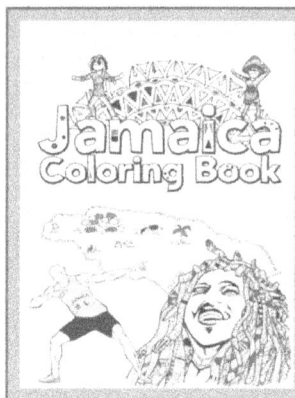

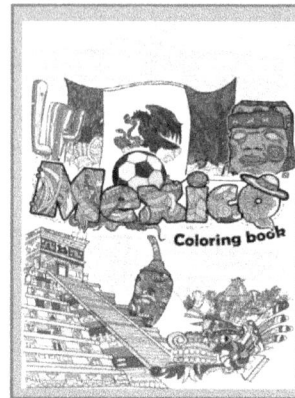

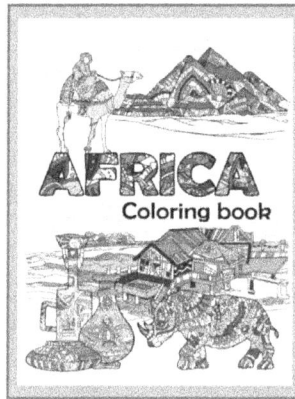

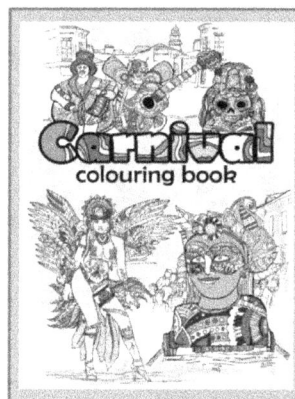

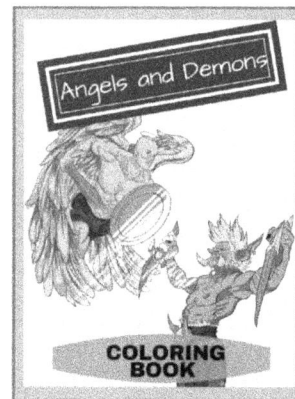

Great Britain
Coloring book

U.S.A.
Coloring book

Jamaica
Coloring Book

Mexico
Coloring book

PIRATE
Coloring Book

Aryla Publishing

DRAGON
Coloring Book

UNICORN
Coloring Book

MERMAIDS
Coloring Book

Black Inventors
Coloring Book

Black History Figures
Coloring Book

AFRICA
Coloring book

Carnival
colouring book

1920'S
COLORING BOOK

Kittens and Puppies
COLORING BOOK

Black Brothers
COLORING BOOK

Angels and Demons
COLORING BOOK

JAPAN

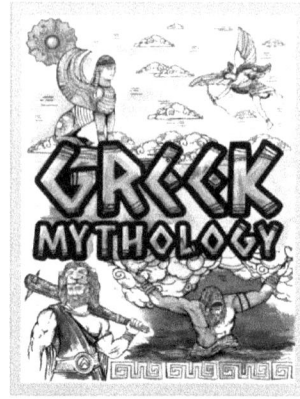
GREEK MYTHOLOGY

BLACK KINGS & QUEENS
COLORING BOOK

BLACK HEROES
Coloring Book

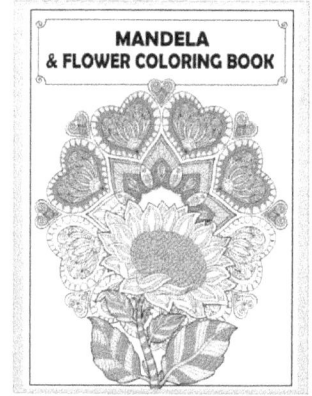
MANDELA & FLOWER COLORING BOOK

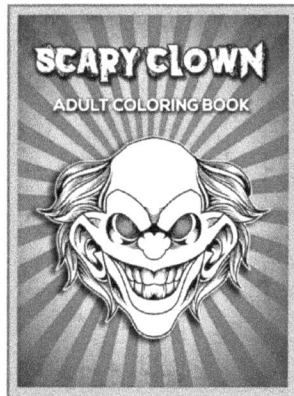
SCARY CLOWN
ADULT COLORING BOOK

CIRCUS
COLORING BOOK

ANIMAL COLORING BOOK

MYTHICAL CREATURES
Coloring Book

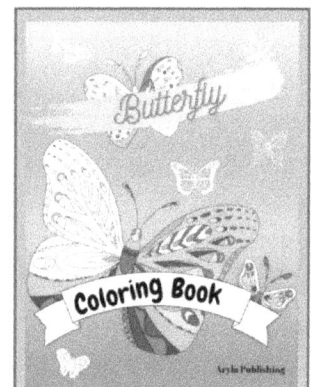
Butterfly
Coloring Book

Visit **www.ArylaPublishing.com**
to find out about all new releases.

Follow us @arylapublishing on Twitter Instagram & Facebook

Search for Aryla Publishing on

YouTube

Check out our Book Trailers

Subscribe to keep up to date with new releases!

WE WOULD LOVE YOUR FEEDBACK

PLEASE LEAVE REVIEW AT:-

www.ingramcontent.com/pod-product-compliance
Lightning Source LLC
Chambersburg PA
CBHW081229020426

42331CB00012B/3101